Akathist
to
Saint Neagoe Basarab

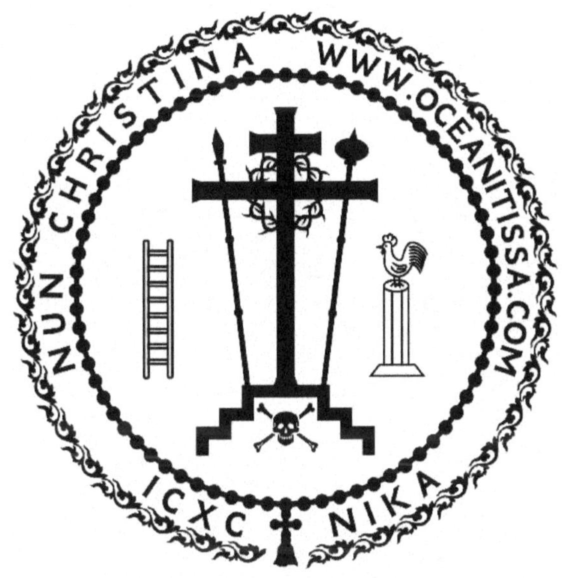

Anna Skoubourdis
Nun Christina

Published by: Virgin Mary of Australia and Oceania 2022 ©
oceanitissa@gmail.com
www.oceanitissa.com.au
Youtube: Nun Christina Oceanitissa

Subscribe to receive updates and Orthodox Christian creative media

www.oceanitissa.com

September 26

The Troparion. Tone 1

Saint Neagoe Voivode, wisest ruler among the leaders of the Romanian people, founder of holy places, friend of the Holy Fathers, teacher enlightened by the Holy Spirit, and a great lover of peace, pray to Christ God to save our souls!

Kontakion 1

With purity in our hearts, let us praise and honor the great Voivode Neagoe Basarab, the one who shone like a light on all sides of Orthodoxy, as a true Christian leader and teacher of the Romanian people, inspired by the Holy Spirit, saying with joy: Rejoice, Saint Neagoe Basarab, fervent intercessor for our souls!

Akathist

Kontakion 1

With purity in our hearts, let us praise and honor the great Voivode Neagoe Basarab, the one who shone like a light on all sides of Orthodoxy, as a true Christian leader and teacher of the Romanian people, inspired by the Holy Spirit, saying with joy: Rejoice, Saint Neagoe Basarab, fervent intercessor for our souls!

Ikos 1

Illustrious son, born of the noble vine of the Romanian nation, Saint Neagoe, from your early childhood, you were nourished with the saving teachings and guided towards the fulfillment of the deeds of faith that work through love pleasing to God and people. For this, we, who commemorate you with holy love, bring you this song:

Rejoice, chosen adornment of the Basarab lineage;
Rejoice, unspeakable joy of your good parents;
Rejoice, pure child strengthened by the grace of the Holy Spirit;
Rejoice, for Christ has placed your soul in uncreated light;
Rejoice, for you were guided by Saint Niphon in your youth;
Rejoice, you who learned to pray from childhood;
Rejoice, for you have drunk the wisdom of the wise;
Rejoice, diligent learner in acquiring the sciences of this world;
Rejoice, for the Holy Scriptures have enlightened your life;
Rejoice, knower and fulfiller of the works of the Holy Fathers;
Rejoice, you who honored the learned monks and zealous Christians;
Rejoice, for the Romanian nation has been blessed through you;
Rejoice, Saint Neagoe Basarab, fervent intercessor for our souls!

Kontakion 2

Just as our Savior Jesus Christ went out to preach the Word of life after the age of thirty, you too completed the acquisition of human and spiritual teachings and, at the same age, you were called to receive the scepter of the reign of a humble and pious people, singing to God: Alleluia!

Ikos 2

Like Moses of old, who led the chosen people to the promised land, taking them out of Pharaoh's enslavement, you too, wise voivode, handled the material goods and the holy desires of your people, always teaching that the promised land is not in the world this, but in heaven. After so many ages, we marvel at your wisdom and the gifts you received from God, singing to you:

Rejoice, perfect voivode among the rulers of the Romanian people;
Rejoice, for Christ was the secret advisor of your soul;
Rejoice, for you had Moses, the friend of God, as an example;
Rejoice, great conqueror, like Emperor Constantine;
Rejoice, worthy descendant of the emperors of bright Byzantium;
Rejoice, symbol of Orthodoxy, pleasing to God;
Rejoice, protector of Christianity in the Balkans and throughout the East;
Rejoice, sun that darkened the crescent;
Rejoice, icon much honored by Orthodox Christians;
Rejoice, you who had the knowledge that your reign is from God;
Rejoice, Christian prince, the one who led the peoples to repentance;
Rejoice, great voivode, dedicated to the service of God and people;
Rejoice, Saint Neagoe, great voivode, teacher of the Romanian nation!

Kontakion 3

As the sun in the sky shines upon both the good and the bad, so were you, faithful voivode, the same for all and different for each throughout your life. Because you did not favor anyone, Saint, but helped the rich and the poor, the monks and ascetics, widows and orphans alike, seeing in each the image of God in the light of similarity, and always giving glory to the Holy Trinity, you sang: Alleluia!

Ikos 3

Saint Neagoe, knowing full well that the dignity and mission of the Christian ruler include the earthly rule, an image of the Kingdom of Heaven, you considered yourself together with Macarius, the Metropolitan of Wallachia, a symbol of the same Christ - Emperor and Hierarch - working all with righteous consideration and humility. That's why we sing to you:

Rejoice, man of God, with the mind enlightened by the Holy Spirit;
Rejoice, you who proved that leading means cultivating souls;
Rejoice, philosopher who separated the science of the vain world from the teaching of Christ;
Rejoice, you who learned the science of leading Christian peoples;
Rejoice, spiritual voivode, image, and likeness of the great emperors;
Rejoice, you who had as a guide in heaven the Emperor Christ and Saint Niphon on earth;
Rejoice, benefactor and protector of the oppressed;
Rejoice, hero of freedom and peacemaker in the Balkans;
Rejoice, friend of the saints and speaker of angels;
Rejoice, Christian voivode, icon of the Eternal King;
Rejoice, Orthodox humanist, bearer of the seal of Byzantine culture;
Rejoice, prince with undiminished dignity, grafted onto the Christ vine;
Rejoice, Saint Neagoe Basarab, fervent intercessor for our souls!

Kontakion 4

Saint Neagoe, the teachings bequeathed to your son Theodosius, and the faithful people, are also a holy call to us to fulfill the spiritually fragrant commandments of the Gospel of Christ and to sing to God, the One praised in the Trinity: Alleluia!

Ikos 4

Great Voivode, you were called most exalted, most brilliant, most pious and most orthodox, as a sage of your times; but we will not call you more than Saint of God and friend of the saints, singing to you:

Rejoice, Christian ruler, lover of peace and well-being;
Rejoice, pen inspired by the grace of the Holy Spirit;
Rejoice, defender of justice and peacemaker of the rebellious;
Rejoice, example of humility and image of the meek;
Rejoice, bringer of peace and joy to people;
Rejoice, you who established holy rules for the Church and rulers;
Rejoice, magnanimous adorner of the holy places;
Rejoice, sower of purity and truth;
Rejoice, care bearer of the afflicted;
Rejoice, preacher of the saving faith;
Rejoice, victor over enemies;
Rejoice, divine harp of Orthodoxy;
Rejoice, morning star that shines in the darkness of ignorance;
Rejoice, Saint Neagoe, great voivode, teacher of the Romanian nation!

Kontakion 5

Saint, all your life, you have shown, by deed and word, that Christian virtues are steps for climbing to God-Love, from Whom comes all good gifts and all justice. That's why, by fasting, praying, keeping your purity, humility, and mercy, you climbed the steps of the spiritual ascent to God, singing: Alleluia!

Ikos 5

Grand voivode, from your advice, we learn that true humanism means the reality of deified humanity, according to the example of Christ. To reach this stage, all your life, you fulfilled the

Decalogue of perfection, which we will also try to fulfill, blessing you and saying:
Rejoice, you who directed your own life according to the commandments of Christ;
Rejoice, for your heart was the abode of uncreated light;
Rejoice, Christian ruler, intercessor for your subjects;
Rejoice, Hesychast prince, bringer of peace to the world;
Rejoice, mouth of gold, who spoke the words of wisdom;
Rejoice, you who did not harm your neighbor;
Rejoice, for you have acquired humble contemplation as the beginning of virtues;
Rejoice, for you did not despise the helpless poor;
Rejoice, leader, who made promises and fulfilled them;
Rejoice, for you have loved God with all your soul and virtue, and your neighbor as yourself;
Rejoice, image of the ruler, true lover of the people;
Rejoice, sharer of the things and troubles of your fellows;
Rejoice, Saint Neagoe Basarab, fervent intercessor for our souls!

Kontakion 6

Faithful voivode, we call you a great founder of holy places and unsurpassed benefactor of many churches and monasteries; for you spared no effort for the dwellings of Christ on earth to shine in beauty and adornment like the luminaries in heaven. For everything, you gave thanks to God, the One who enriched you with heavenly gifts, singing: Alleluia!

Ikos 6

"The Father built this house, the Son renewed this house, the Holy Spirit enlightened this house, and sanctified our souls" was sung at the consecration of the Romanian Zion in Argeş, Saint Neagoe. Therefore, Master Manole, the builder of the abode of the Most Holy Theotokos, is none other than Emmanuel Himself, God the Most Eternal. Wonderful are Your works, Lord, for You have done them all with wisdom!

Rejoice, founder of the Romanian Zion from Argeş;
Rejoice, for the fame of his beauty has spread throughout the world;
Rejoice, you who gave God a bouquet of spiritual flowers;
Rejoice, for your church is the gate of heaven and the house of God;
Rejoice, for Saint Philofteia dwells in the church you founded;
Rejoice, you who endowed the church of your burial with expensive ornaments;
Rejoice, for many marvel at this house of God;
Rejoice, for your abode has become the eternal resting place of many rulers;
Rejoice, you who carved in stone the history of your nation;
Rejoice, for the greatness of this church has been preserved over the ages;
Rejoice, for you have also built your holy abode in the heavens;
Rejoice, for God has accepted the sacrifice of your labors;
Rejoice, Saint Neagoe, great voivode, teacher of the Romanian nation!

Kontakion 7

A great celebration was held at the consecration of the Argeş parish in honor of the Blessed Virgin Mary; all the abbots of the Holy Mountain, led by Patriarch Theolipt of Constantinople along with priests and elected people, went to this holy celebration, according to the Holy Traditions. Everyone marveled at the unspeakable beauty of the church founded by you, faithful voivode, singing to God: Alleluia!

Ikos 7

Saint Neagoe, you ordained that, if the consecration of the church where your body would rest is completed, that building would remain a place of peace and prayer for monks and pilgrims, for you moved the country's Metropolis to Târgovişte, where again you built a great church, thanking God, and we sing to you:

Rejoice, pride of Targoviște and the entire Romanian nation;
Rejoice, founder of the Metropolitan Church of Wallachia;
Rejoice, reconciler of Saint Niphon with Radu Voivode;
Rejoice, for you have performed miracles through true faith;
Rejoice, adorner of the holy relics of your spiritual father;
Rejoice, innovative founder of the Dionysius Lavra and other Athonite monasteries;
Rejoice, for you also renewed monasteries and churches in Serbia;
Rejoice, conferrer of many holy places throughout Orthodoxy;
Rejoice, for not a single church in your country was without help;
Rejoice, you who established laws and traditions for the churched you founded;
Rejoice, for no one can tell your many deeds in the name of Christ;
Rejoice, Saint Neagoe Basarab, fervent intercessor for our souls!

Kontakion 8

Saint Neagoe, great voivode, keeping the right faith, completing the path, you appeared with the tree of your life loaded with the deeds of faith at the end of your earthly life before the Just Redeemer, Who gifted you the royal crown of eternal life, placing you in the company of Christian emperors to sing: Alleluia!

Ikos 8

Wanting to show the world that those who love the adornment of God's House and fulfill His will here on earth do not labor in vain, Christ glorified Saint Neagoe with much honor at his passing from this transitory life, placing him in His eternal rest, from where he prays for us, those who sing to him:

Rejoice, Saint voivode, you who had your thoughts to death and your mind raised to God;
Rejoice, you who left the valley of mourning ahead of time;
Rejoice, for Christ has announced to you the hour of the end;
Rejoice, for the angels ministered at your feast;
Rejoice, for you had a good and Christian end;

Rejoice, you who knew that the souls of the righteous are in the hand of God and torment will not touch them;
Rejoice, for your soul has become clear like gold in the furnace;
Rejoice, for you have hoped in God, who has revealed His wonders to you;
Rejoice, for love for Him has consumed you all your life;
Rejoice, for you have found mercy and grace before the Right Judge;
Rejoice, the one full of triune and gentle light;
Rejoice, intercessor for the faithful Romanian people;
Rejoice, Saint Neagoe, great voivode, teacher of the Romanian nation!

Kontakion 9

Your body, Saint Neagoe, full of the fragrance of virtues, was buried with honor in the Church of the Mother of God, which you built, and your soul was placed by Christ the Savior, Whom you loved, in the garden of the paradise of delight, where you see God face to face, to Whom you sing: Alleluia!

Ikos 9

We know from the Holy Scriptures that nothing unclean enters the Kingdom of God, and Tradition adds: No creator enters eternity except by carrying on his shoulders the seal of his life. You, Saint Neagoe, are one of these, for Christ recognized Himself in your face and the deeds you performed here on earth for His glory. That's why we sing to you:

Rejoice, burning candle from the light of Christ;
Rejoice, you who rejoice together with the hosts of angels;
Rejoice, you who delight with the saints, friends, and household of God;
Rejoice, you who always see the face of the One whom you served;
Rejoice, for you ascend from glory to glory to the mystery of the Holy Trinity;
Rejoice, for you dwell in unspeakable light in heaven;

Rejoice, you who discovered the Mysteries of God;
Rejoice, for many lights are burning around you;
Rejoice, for your being is permeated with the fragrance of grace;
Rejoice, for your life was like a Holy Liturgy;
Rejoice, for you commune from immaterial food;
Rejoice, you who thank God for everything you have received;
Rejoice, Saint Neagoe Basarab, fervent intercessor for our souls!

Kontakion 10

Drinking from the source of the uncreated lights of heaven, you became a source of blessing for us, and through you, we contemplate the ray of the light of the thrice-brilliant divinity and learn to sing: Alleluia!

Ikos 10

Saint Neagoe, cultivating on earth the field of souls in which God invisibly dripped from His grace, it produced the fruits of the Holy Spirit, and to you, who are in heaven, we thank you for the zeal of the accomplished work, and we honor you, saying:

Rejoice, rare flower of the Romanian garden, planted in the heaven of delight;
Rejoice, sweet-smelling rose with petals in the uncreated light;
Rejoice, bright-rayed and ever-living aurora;
Rejoice, mind full of the fragrance of good teachings;
Rejoice, inner eye that sees things unseen by us;
Rejoice, blessed voivode, the adornment of the Romanian lands;
Rejoice, seer of the divine mysteries of heaven;
Rejoice, most beautiful icon of all Orthodoxy;
Rejoice, precious stone cut from the Christ stone;
Rejoice, pearl that adorns the sky;
Rejoice, heavenly light burning for eternity;
Rejoice, ladder of accomplished virtues on which we climb to the heavens;
Rejoice, Saint Neagoe, great voivode, teacher of the Romanian nation!

Kontakion 11

Faithful voivode of the Romanian nation, Saint Neagoe Basarab, climbing into the chariot of virtues, you ascended to the unspeakable beauty of the Kingdom of Heaven. Pray, beloved of God, that we may be saved and teach us to sing to God: Alleluia!

Ikos 11

Great voivode, Saint Neagoe, tireless intercessor for the nation from which you came, ask Christ to grant us His mercy and wisdom, peace, and great compassion to our souls so that we can sing:

Rejoice, helper of those fallen in the whirlwind of hardships;
Rejoice, relief of bodily and soul pains;
Rejoice, healer of the unhealed diseases;
Rejoice, giver of wisdom to eager youth;
Rejoice, protector of widows and helper of orphans;
Rejoice, gentle father, supporter of the poor;
Rejoice, bearer of the balm of healings;
Rejoice, guide of pilgrims and travelers;
Rejoice, bringer of peace and abundance;
Rejoice, adorner of churches and monasteries;
Rejoice, hope of the hopeless;
Rejoice, supporter of the weary and consolation of the unfortunate;
Rejoice, Saint Neagoe Basarab, fervent intercessor for our souls!

Kontakion 12

Saint Neagoe, you are a light-carrying torch for the faithful Romanian nation, for even now, you illuminate its paths and strengthen its Church so that it can overcome the traps of its seen and unseen enemies. We thank God for we have you as a caretaker and light of the nation, singing to Him: Alleluia!

Ikos 12

Come, all the sons of the Romanian nation, and let us praise the wise among voivods, Saint Neagoe Besarab, who for centuries has been calling us to worship the Most Holy Trinity, our God, to take care of the garden of the Mother of God and to honor the saints, following their teachings, saying:

Rejoice, wall of peace and tranquility for the Romanian nation;
Rejoice, the joy of the people of Argeș and the praise of Târgoviște;
Rejoice, oak grown in the Garden of the Mother of God;
Rejoice, guardian who watches over the Romanian lands;
Rejoice, destroyer of heresies and vain teachings;
Rejoice, fervent supplicant for all Christendom;
Rejoice, teacher of the learned, and example of rulers;
Rejoice, porphyry that adorns the Orthodox Church;
Rejoice, treasury full of spiritual delights;
Rejoice, quick help to those who honor your name;
Rejoice, our support in the time of the end;
Rejoice, ladder to heaven of those seeking salvation;
Rejoice, Saint Neagoe, great voivode, teacher of the Romanian nation!

Kontakion 13

O wise voivode, Saint Neagoe Basarab, accept this humble prayer that we bring to you with pure hearts, we, the sons of the Romanian nation whom you loved, and deliver us from all the toils and temptations of life, asking God to save our souls so that we can sing to Him with you: Alleluia! (*Repeat this kontakion three times.*)

Repeat ikos 1 and kontakion 1.

Ikos 1
Illustrious son, born of the noble vine of the Romanian nation, Saint Neagoe, from your early childhood, you were nourished with the saving teachings and guided towards the fulfillment of the

deeds of faith that work through love pleasing to God and people. For this, we, who commemorate you with holy love, bring you this song:

Rejoice, chosen adornment of the Basarab lineage;
Rejoice, unspeakable joy of your good parents;
Rejoice, pure child strengthened by the grace of the Holy Spirit;
Rejoice, for Christ has placed your soul in uncreated light;
Rejoice, for you were guided by Saint Niphon in your youth;
Rejoice, you who learned to pray from childhood;
Rejoice, for you have drunk the wisdom of the wise;
Rejoice, diligent learner in acquiring the sciences of this world;
Rejoice, for the Holy Scriptures have enlightened your life;
Rejoice, knower and fulfiller of the works of the Holy Fathers;
Rejoice, you who honored the learned monks and zealous Christians;
Rejoice, for the Romanian nation has been blessed through you;
Rejoice, Saint Neagoe Basarab, fervent intercessor for our souls!

Kontakion 1

With purity in our hearts, let us praise and honor the great Voivode Neagoe Basarab, the one who shone like a light on all sides of Orthodoxy, as a true Christian leader and teacher of the Romanian people, inspired by the Holy Spirit, saying with joy: Rejoice, Saint Neagoe Basarab, fervent intercessor for our souls!

Prayer to Saint Voivode Neagoe Basarab

Our Lord, the God of mercies and all compassions, the wonderful One among Your saints and whose prayers You listen to, receive our request that we bring to You on the day of the celebration of Your friend and householder, Neagoe Basarab. You, Lord, have ordained for our nation, in all times and places, where Your name is glorified, heroes of the faith and saints who have pleased You from generation to generation, among which the great Voivode Neagoe Basarab shines. For his prayers, pour out Your beneficent peace and tranquility on all of us so that we may each overcome the hardships and temptations of life: send righteous wisdom to our rulers, the image of holiness to our hierarchs, the fulfillment of the mission to which to the priests, patience, and humility to the monks, and faithful protection and help in times of trouble to the people so that we all glorify You, the Father, the Son, and the Holy Spirit, the Trinity of one being and inseparable, forever and ever. Amen.

Dismissal prayer.

Biography

In the 16th century, Wallachia was independent, but was required to pay an exorbitant tribute to the greater force of the Ottoman Empire. Neagoe encouraged the development of crafts and trade, while maintaining a good relation with Wallachia's other powerful neighbour, Hungary.

His diplomacy attempted to establish connections with the Republic of Venice and the Papacy, even offering to mediate the dispute between Eastern Orthodoxy and Roman Catholicism, with the purpose of uniting Christendom against the Ottoman threat.

He adopted the Byzantine tradition of Church patronage, making generous donations to the Orthodox monasteries, not only in Wallachia but throughout the Balkans. During his reign the Curtea de Argeş Monastery was built (in 1517) – legend names Meşterul Manole as the chief craftsman; the account also fuses Neagoe with yet another legendary figure, Prince Radu (who would've caused Manole's death by ordering for the scaffolding to be removed while the builders were on the roof, ensuring that nobody would use Manole's craft, and thus preserving the uniqueness of the structure).

Neagoe ordered the earliest works on the old Metropolitan church in Târgovişte (the city where the edition of the Gospels was published in 1512) and St. Nicholas Church in Şcheii Braşovului.

Neagoe Basarab wrote in Church Slavonic one of the earliest literary works of Wallachia, called "The teachings of Neagoe Basarab to his son Theodosie" (translated in Romanian as Învăţăturile lui Neagoe Basarab către fiul său Teodosie), where he touches various subjects such as philosophy, diplomacy, morals and ethics.

From another source:

Between 1512 and 1521, Prince Neagoe Basarab was the ruler of Wallachia—the Romanian principality extending to the south of the Carpathian Mountains and north of the Danube River in modern Romania. In 1505, Neagoe married Milica Despina of Serbia—a descendant of the houses of Branković and Lazarević—and together they had six children. There are few extant images of Neagoe Basarab and his family. A less known composition of the group is preserved on the inside lid of a wooden box now in the collection of Saint Catherine Monastery on Mount Sinai. The indentations of where the hardware once attached the lid to the box remain visible on the object, so clearly the image in the central composition once decorated the inside of the lid of a wooden chest.

The painting shows eight kneeling figures in prayer directing their attention toward the central upper portion of the composition where an image of the Virgin Mary with the Christ Child in a heavenly sphere fixates their attention and that of the viewer. The image of the Virgin and Christ is that of the Blachernitissa type with roots in the icon from the Church of the Blachernai in Constantinople (now Istanbul). It generally shows the Virgin half-length and with both her hands raised to either side—in an orans gesture—and with the Christ Child upon her bosom. Christ directs his blessing toward the faithful, and the Virgin, in turn, intercedes on their behalf. In the lower portion of the Sinai panel, the eight kneeling figures are divided into two groups: the men on the left and the women on the right. The distinct features and garments of the figures, as well as the inscriptions in Church Slavonic above their heads, helps identify them. On the left, the image displays Neagoe Basarab (d. 1521) and his three sons: Theodosius, Peter, and John. On the right is his wife, Milica Despina (d. 1554), and their daughters: Stana, Ruxandra, and Angelina. The panel preserves a unique image of this royal family.

The image on the Sinai lid resembles closely the votive mural of Neagoe and his family painted on the interior of the Church of the Dormition of the Virgin at Curtea de Argeș Monastery in Romania. The image shows all eight members of the Basarab family standing and offering a model of the very church in which they are depicted to an image of the Virgin and Child in the heavens above similar to the one found on the Sinai panel. The features and garments of the figures in both family portraits resemble each other, suggesting that the painting on the Sinai lid is contemporaneous with the votive image at Curtea de Argeș.

During his reign, Prince Neagoe Basarab was concerned with the proper education of his heirs. Therefore, he penned the little-known but important text titled *The Teachings of Neagoe Basarab to His Son Theodosius*. This is an unparalleled *speculum principum* written in Church Slavonic in the Eastern Orthodox cultural sphere, contemporaneous with, yet divergent in its ideologies from, Machiavelli's political treatise *The Prince* (*De Principatibus*, 1513; published 1532). As the oldest among the sons, Theodosius succeeded his father to the throne on September 15, 1521. Due to his young age at the time, his mother, Milica, acted as his regent. Unfortunately, Theodosius died only a few months after taking the crown, in January 1522. Little is known of Neagoe and Milica's other two sons, Peter and John. As for the daughters, it is known that Stana married Moldavia's prince Stephen IV (r. 1517–1527), and Ruxandra married Radu of Afumați, who took control of Wallachia after Theodosius's death (r. 1522–1529).

As a ruler of an Orthodox land in the decades after the fall of Constantinople in 1453, Neagoe Basarab fostered relations with the monastic communities on Mount Athos—the pan-Orthodox community of Christians that served as an enduring emblem of Eastern Christianity. It is known that Neagoe made monetary donations and gifted precious icons, manuscripts, embroideries, and metalwork to the Athonite monasteries. His efforts renew for those communities the objects needed for the celebration of the liturgy and ensured his remembrance among the local monks. His deeds aligned with the long tradition of patronage of Athos among the rulers of the north-Danubian principalities—a tradition that began during the second half of the fourteenth century and intensified after the fall of the Byzantine Empire. This is especially evident in the Athonite patronage of Moldavia's ruler Prince Stephen III (r. 1457–1504), for example.

Books published by Nun Christina Oceanitissa:

The collective works of St Nektarios of Aegina.
The Philokalia 5: The full text in English.
The collective works of Elder Cleopa.
The Anacreontic Poems by Saint Sophronius Patriarch of Jerusalem.
The Life of Saint Paul of Thebes the First Hermit.
The Devil: The Cause of Sin by Saint John of Kronstadt.
Faith and the Orthodox Church by Saint John of Kronstadt.
The Monastic Rule of Saint Pachomius the Great.
Supplicatory Canon and Akathist to St Paisios.
Supplicatory Canon and Akathist to St Porphyrios.
Supplicatory Canon and Akathist to St George.
Supplicatory Canon and Akathist to St Anastasia.
Supplicatory Canon and Akathist to St Anna.
Supplicatory Canon and Akathist to St John the Russian.
Supplicatory Canon and Akathist to St Ephraim of Nea Makri.
Supplicatory Canon and Akathist to St John Maximovitch.
Supplicatory Canon and Akathist to St Dimitri.
Supplicatory Canon and Akathist to St Joseph the Hesycast.
Supplicatory Canon and Akathist to St Luke the Surgeon.
Supplicatory Canon and Akathist to St John the Baptist.
The Way of a Pilgrim.
Conversation with a Grieving Man by St Dimitri of Rostov.
The Inner Man by St Dimitri of Rostov.
Orthodox Prayer Book.
Daily Orthodox Prayer book.

www.ingramcontent.com/pod-product-compliance
Lightning Source LLC
LaVergne TN
LVHW010512160826
845677LV00012B/2805

* 9 7 9 8 8 4 8 4 8 3 4 9 9 *